pRay the WORd

for YOUR CHURCH

31 PRAYERS THAT SEEK GOD'S PURPOSES *and* POWER

TIECE L. KING

PRAYERSHOP PUBLISHING

Terre Haute, Indiana

Greg Hiday

PrayerShop Publishing is the publishing arm of Harvest Prayer Ministries and the Church Prayer Leaders Network. Harvest Prayer Ministries exists to transform lives through teaching prayer. Its online prayer store, www.prayershop.org, has more than 400 prayer resources available for purchase.

ISBN: 978-1-935012-62-7

This resource contains Scripture-based prayers. Each prayer is filled with thoughts based on specific verses. Only short phrases appear that are taken from various versions. That is why we do not cite a particular version of the Bible beyond the version used in the main Scripture of each prayer.

1 2 3 4 5 | 2019 2018 2017 2016 2015

Table of Contents

Foreword

Prayer isn't a Christian's *only* responsibility, but if it doesn't become a *primary* responsibility then we're not being responsible Christians. Prayerless Christianity is fruitless Christianity.

Jesus prayed. Jesus taught us to pray. Jesus continues to pray for us. How could we do any less?

However, prayer doesn't come naturally for many of us.

When I was young, my sisters tried to get me to talk. Talk? It felt so foreign. *Doing* came easily. *Talking* was learned behavior. Then I was called to become a pastor—a calling that required me to use words regularly. Still, I'd prefer to be on the listening end than the one speaking.

Meanwhile, I am invited by our loving God to talk with Him. I like the listening part, but often—quiet guy that I am—I am at a loss for words. This is one reason that the resources Ty King is providing have become of great value to me. Often when I wanted to put words to prayer but have come up short, I've turned to *Pray the Word*. I've appreciated each prayer—clearly arising from Holy Scripture—helping me articulate my heart.

Now, with her second volume, *Pray the Word for Your Church*, Ty welcomes us into another prayer journey. I commend it not only to personalities like mine but also to all the Body of Christ. Theologically rich, bursting with Scripture, thoughtfully written, worthy of reflection and faith-enlarging, this is a prayer tool that many sincere Jesus-followers will turn to again and again.

I consider it an honor to know Ty and David, her husband, personally. Their lives inspire me to love, live, and pray with greater joy and fervency. I've also been a firsthand witness of the significant impact that the ministry of prayer is having in the church that the Kings serve, the Evangelical Church of Bangkok (ECB). Powerful worship, anointed preaching, and city-impacting ministry are the common experiences of ECB as a direct result of the intentional, passionate, faith-filled, Scripture-based prayer that is foundational to the church. Prayer isn't the only ministry of ECB, but it shapes and prepares the way for every ministry.

Together for His Kingdom,
Dr. John Stumbo
President, U.S. Christian & Missionary Alliance

Introduction

Perhaps the cry of Habakkuk's heart resonates with you as well:

"LORD, I have heard of your fame;
I stand in awe of your deeds, LORD.
Repeat them in our day,
in our time make them known." Habakkuk 3:2

It was two decades ago that God laid a burden upon me in prayer for the revival of His Church and a "Habakkuk longing" in me was birthed. Suddenly my prayers were fueled with fresh visions of dead bones coming to life, hard hearts broken open and new streams flowing in desert places. As I prayed, I became more and more convinced that prayer truly is our only hope. Too often we measure our churches by the length of our budgets, the breadth of our facilities and the height of our attendance—but too little by the depth of prayer that reflects the condition of our hearts. All the church growth strategies, plans, and programs cannot change the hearts of men and women. Only the Holy Spirit poured out, gifting the people of God with brokenness, repentance, and a desire to be like Jesus, will revive the dead and dusty places and bring lasting change that produces new life and light.

However I must tell you that in calling people to pray the heart of God for the Church, there is one thing that I've seen over and over again (and perhaps you've experienced this as well). When prayer is lifted before the Throne for renewal and change in church communities, the work of the Spirit first begins in the heart of each petitioner. Remember, *we* are the Church. And so in praying for your faith community, you are praying for the work of the Holy Spirit in your own heart as well. May revival begin with you and me.

The prayers in this book are based on the Word of God, for the people of God. I encourage you to take your time to make these prayers your own. Savor them and pray them from your heart. Insert names of people in your church community, petition God on behalf of your pastors—allow the Holy Spirit to pray through you and fuel your prayers with fresh passion for more of Jesus.

There are additional prayer pages in the back of this book for listing names, ministries, and special prayer burdens. I encourage you to use them to further saturate your community of faith in prayer.

The world is waiting for, and in desperate need of, a vibrant alive-in-Jesus Church. Surely it is time for another "great awakening"! May we be those who, through prayer, remove the obstacles out of the way of God's people and prepare the way of the Lord.

Dear brothers and sisters, let us always pray and never give up.

—Ty King

Ezekiel 37:9-10; Jeremiah 23:29; Isaiah 43:19; Isaiah 57:14; Luke 18:1

A Proclamation:
Jesus Is Head over All

Consider praying this prayer out loud as a declaration of praise.

*And [Jesus] is head of the body the church, the beginning and
the firstborn from among the dead so that in everything he
might have the supremacy. Colossians 1:18*

Lord Jesus Christ, this day I pronounce over (name of your church) that *You rule over all.* You alone are head of the body, Your Church. You are Lord over all—supreme in all things! For God the Father was pleased to have all His fullness dwell in You, Lord Jesus, and through You, to reconcile all things to Yourself. *All things*—on earth and in heaven. You have brought everything near through Your blood shed on the cross, You the Righteous One for the unrighteous, that we might be brought into the family of God!

Once, we were totally separated from the Father. We were orphaned, enemies in our minds because of our wickedness. We were without hope and without God. But now, because of Your finished work on the cross, we have been reconciled to God, presented as holy—spotless! Strengthen us by Your Spirit I pray, to live out this mystery.

May we as Your people choose to humble ourselves before You and submit to Your Word. Destroy pride, self-righteousness and all strongholds of self-reliance among us.

May I and my brothers and sisters in Christ be strengthened to stand firm this day and walk in the great victory of the cross. May we be established and unmovable—always clinging to the hope of the gospel, and unaffected by the lies of the accuser. For Jesus Christ, You alone are Lord, to the glory of God the Father, and *we are Yours!*

This day as a member of Your Body, the Church, I choose to humble myself under Your lordship and I proclaim that You are head over all.

Jesus, You are Lord over Your Church. *(Pause and pray for your brothers and sisters around the world. Pray that the global Church of Jesus Christ will be strengthened and revived.)*

Jesus, You are Lord over my church community. *(Pause and pray for your faith community.)*

Jesus, You are Lord over my life. *(Pause and submit yourself once again to the lordship of Jesus.)*

Lord Jesus, I make this confession in Your mighty name, the Name above all names, *Jesus the Christ, the Son of the Living God.* Amen and AMEN!

Psalm 24:1, 103:19; Hebrews 1:3; Colossians 1:15-23; Acts 10:36; 1 Corinthians 15:20-21; 1 Peter 3:18; Ephesians 2:12; Philippians 2:11; Matthew 16:18

Proclaiming Jesus

You will receive power when the Holy Spirit comes on you;
and you will be my witnesses in Jerusalem, and in all Judea
and Samaria, and to the ends of the earth. Acts 1:8

Heavenly Father, as I quiet my heart before You, I confess that *Jesus is Lord* and there is salvation in no one else. It is through Your name alone that I have been saved and the people of the world will receive salvation! O God, forgive me for the ways that I have kept this good news to myself. *(Be still before the Lord.)*

This day I ask, Lord, for a fresh *empowering* of the Holy Spirit on my life and the lives of my brothers and sisters in Christ in my church community, that our hearts might be captured with a new urgency to be gospel proclaimers.

May a longing to see souls come to know You increase among us, I pray!

May the message of reconciliation that has been committed to us be released through our lives and be upon our lips that we might truly live as ambassadors of Christ. *(Pray for those in your life by name, who do not yet know Jesus.)*

May the beauty of Jesus increase in our lives as we bring good news and blessing into our conversations. May every task we encounter provide opportunity for gospel conversations with those around us.

May the peace of Christ so rest upon us that our presence and Jesus-proclamations in the world are a healing balm of peace for every troubled heart.

May all fear of rejection be banished from our lives! Instead may we increasingly be those who are always prepared to give the reason for the hope that we have. May timidity be replaced with a gentle, holy boldness that the message of salvation might be proclaimed through us with great love.

May we be filled with fresh faith and a deepening confidence, that in spite of all that we see or hear around us, *our God reigns!* And You rule over all! May our trust in You and hope in Your name increasingly be part of the conversations of our lives.

I ask, Father, that whenever I open my mouth, Your words would be given to me so that I might make known the mystery of the gospel without fear. *(Pause and ask that all fear and timidity in your life be destroyed.)* O God, may the Holy Spirit be present in power among us and may our community of faith grow through new believers! Add to our number daily those who are being saved. *(Pause and pray for spiritual harvest in your church community.)*

Surely, Lord Jesus, You are coming soon! May we be found faithfully engaging in the work of Your kingdom as gospel-proclaimers. From our "Jerusalem" to the "ends of the earth," may the good news of Jesus be made known with great joy and those who are in darkness, come into the Light! In Jesus' name alone. Amen and amen!

Romans 10:9; Acts 4:12; 2 Corinthians 5:18-21; Isaiah 52:7; Colossians 3:15; Romans 8:6; 1 Peter 3:15; 2 Timothy 1:7; Ephesians 6:19; Romans 10:14-15; Acts 2:47, 1:8; Luke 2:10

Being Filled with the Holy Spirit

Be filled with the [Holy] Spirit. Ephesians 5:18

Father, how thankful I am for the seal of the Holy Spirit on my life, His deposit in my heart that testifies that I am truly Yours. But today, Father, I come asking for more. Fill me afresh, I pray, with the presence and power of the Holy Spirit. *(Bring your heart before the Lord. Ask for a fresh infilling of the Holy Spirit.)*

I ask for myself and my brothers and sisters at (name of church), that we would be increasingly radical in putting to death our sinful natures that the lordship of Jesus might be firmly established in our living, and there be greater room for the work of the Holy Spirit in our hearts. O God, may we be clothed with power from on high! Make us ready to receive all that You have for us, I pray.

Forgive us, Father, for the plans that we have made and the ways that we have walked in our own strength and have ignored the Holy Spirit. In doing so, we have put out the Spirit's fire. Have mercy, Lord, and fill us again with the Holy Spirit.

I pray for our pastor(s) and ask that they would lead us by the Holy Spirit into deeper waters. Pour out Your Holy Spirit on them, I pray, with a fresh anointing to live out their calling. *(Pray for your pastor(s) by name.)*

I ask for our elders, deacons, and council members. Oh God, may all things be accomplished through the leading of, and submission to, the Holy Spirit. In all ways and in all things, may selfish ambition be put to death and the life of the Spirit unleashed in the hearts of those who lead us!

As we gather to worship together, I ask that the Holy Spirit rain down on us that we might be changed and first-love passion for Jesus burn within us once again. I ask that the Holy Spirit be present in power among us, from youngest to oldest. O God, fill us to overflowing with the Holy Spirit. *(Pause and pray for those in your church community whom you know by name. Ask that the Holy Spirit be poured out on their lives.)*

May we be led and guided by the Holy Spirit into ever deeper truth that we might truly know Christ and make Him known. Increase our hunger for Your Word and for holiness and the fullness of the expression of the Spirit among us.

May we learn to live by the Spirit in our everyday living, being attentive to His voice and obedient to His promptings.

May we keep in step with the Holy Spirit, putting aside our own agendas, watching closely for where He is at work, and eagerly entering in.

May the fruit of the Spirit increase in our lives causing us to overflow with love, joy, peace, patience, kindness, goodness, faithfulness, gentleness, and self-control. May it be evident to all that we belong to You.

Through the continual filling of the Holy Spirit, change us, O God, and in so doing, may Your church come alive and be revived. In Jesus' name I ask. Amen.

---

2 Corinthians 1:22; Luke 11:13, 24:49; 1 Samuel 2:9; Zechariah 4:6; 1 Thessalonians 5:19; John 16:13; Galatians 5:16,25,22

Choosing Humility

Be completely humble and gentle; be patient, bearing with one another in love. Ephesians 4:2

Heavenly Father, Your Word admonishes us to clothe ourselves with humility toward one another, that You oppose the proud but give grace to those who are humble. By the work of the Holy Spirit in our hearts, teach my church community this way of living out Christ with one another. May we (*may I, Lord*) put aside our self-serving ways and choose to consider each other's needs first.

May each and every one in my fellowship of believers be determined to keep the unity of the Spirit. Father, I ask that You destroy all gossip, envy, and strife that is yet among us. Keep us from judging one another.

Father, I ask in the name of the Lord Jesus Christ that the stronghold of pride be broken among us, and all the ways that it is evident in our living be destroyed.

> From our need to be right and our opinions to be validated, O Lord, save us.
>
> From our prejudices and preferences, O Lord, save us.
>
> From our sense of entitlement, O Lord, deliver us.

For our refusal to serve and use our gifts for Your kingdom purposes, O God, forgive us.

For our lack of repentance and brokenness before You, O God, have mercy on us.

(Pause and ask the Holy Spirit to show you where these things might be evident in your own life and confess them to the Lord.)

It is written, Father, that the sacrifices that please You are a broken and contrite heart, and so I ask in agreement with Your Word that we might become a people marked by repentance and humility before You. May the very meditations of our hearts be brought under the rule and reign of the Holy Spirit and every thought that keeps us ensnared in prideful living be taken captive in Jesus' name.

Teach us as a church community to follow the example of Jesus, our Lord and Master, Who humbled Himself and became a servant, washing the feet of those He led. Strengthen us by the Holy Spirit to follow His example, that our relationships with one another might also be defined by "towel and basin" humility. May we serve each other out of love for Christ.

O God, help us in our weakness. Teach us to walk in Your way that as a community of faith we might move forward in humility together in the kingdom work that You have for us. In Jesus' name. Amen.

---

1 Peter 5:5; Philippians 2:3-4; Ephesians 4:3; Galatians 5:19-21; John 7:24; James 1:19; Proverbs 10:19; James 2:14; Luke 18:9-14; 1 Corinthians 12:4-7; Psalm 50:17, 19:14; 2 Corinthians 10:5; John 13:12-17; 2 Corinthians 12:9; Psalm 86:11

Putting on the Armor of God

*Put on the full armor of God, so that you can take your stand
against the devil's schemes. Ephesians 6:11*

Father, You have called Your Church to be strong in You
and in Your mighty power—not our own strength—but the
resurrection power of Christ. O God, have mercy on us and forgive us
(*forgive me*), for too often we have gone our own way and depended on
ourselves, our resources, and the wisdom of man rather than depend
on You. We have not stood in the victory of the Lord Jesus Christ.

This day, Father, I acknowledge that the battles in my life, and the
lives of my brothers and sisters in Christ Jesus, are not against what is
seen, but against what is unseen—all spiritual forces of evil in heavenly
places. O God, remind us continually, by the presence of the Holy
Spirit in each of us, to put on Christ that we might be able to stand
our ground against the enemy of our souls.

This day, Father, I proclaim over Your Church, my faith community
and my life:

> Lord Jesus Christ, You are the way and the *truth* and
> the life. May Your Church turn from all false teaching and
> philosophies of this world and walk in the truth of Your

Word. Be the belt of Truth around us this day.

May we turn from all sin that entangles us and walk in the righteousness that You have provided, Lord Jesus. You Who became sin for us, You are our breastplate of righteousness.

Make us ready to give the reason for the hope that we have, Lord! May our feet be fitted with the gospel of peace. Jesus, I confess that You are the good news. You are our peace.

May all of the attacks of the evil one that come against Your people be extinguished as faith rises up in our hearts. Lord Jesus, shield us in faith.

Lord Jesus Christ, I proclaim that salvation is found in no one else, for there is no name under heaven other than Yours, by which we can be saved from sin! You, Lord Jesus, are the Christ, the Son of the Living God. You are our salvation.

This day, may the Word dwell richly in the hearts of Your Church. May it accomplish all that You intend, convicting of sin, judging attitudes and actions, revealing Jesus, defining the very way we live. Teach us to follow Your example, Lord Jesus, and take up this Sword and do battle!

In all things, I choose to put on Christ this day and take my stand. May I be ready, alert, and faithful in prayer. In Your name, Lord Jesus, I ask for my brothers and sisters as well. May they be strengthened by the Holy Spirit to do the same, that Your work in us this day might be *mighty*.

I ask all these things in the name of Jesus, Who gave Himself for us that we might share in His authority and be *more than* conquerors. Amen and AMEN!

Ephesians 6:10, 1:19-20; Jeremiah 17:5; Ephesians 6:11-18; Hebrews 12:2;
2 Corinthians 5:21; 1 Peter 3:15; Acts 4:12; Matthew 16:16; Colossians 3:16; Isaiah 55:11; Hebrews 4:12; John 1:14; Matthew 4:4-10; Ephesians 1:22, 2:6; Romans 8:37

Understanding the Father's Love

[May you] know this love that surpasses knowledge.
Ephesians 3:19

Heavenly Father, I come to You this day in prayer on behalf of my church community, choosing to humble myself before You as Your child. I ask, Father, that according to Your great richness, strengthen us with power through the Holy Spirit at the core of our being.

May Jesus Christ truly dwell in our hearts in all of His fullness. May each of us (*may I*) break up the unplowed ground that yet remains in our hearts, that faith might grow and increase.

May the root of love grow deep in us—love for You, love for one another, love for those who have yet to call on Your name. Establish us firmly in Your love.

May we receive power from the Holy Spirit to understand, with greater depth and meaning ,Your immeasurable love for us expressed through Christ! For Your love is higher than the heavens are above the earth and wider than the east is from the west. Help us in our weakness to understand this mystery in such a way that it changes us from the inside out.

May we be filled up with more of You. Push out self-focused living that has taken up space in our hearts that belongs to You alone.

Replace it, I pray, with the fullness of Christ, that we might overflow with His love. May we increasingly live and move and have our very being in Him.

How thankful I am, Father, that nothing is too hard for You. You are the God of the impossible, the improbable—able to do more than I can ask for or imagine! Forgive me for my faithless praying and the smallness of my heart. I ask for a fresh realization of Your greatness and glory that causes faith to rise up within me once again, birthing God-sized dreams. For it is Your power that is at work in me—it is Your faithful love that always endures. *(Pray for your community of faith, your pastor(s), and those you know by name, that these things would become true of them as well.)*

May the glory of Jesus be evident in my church community this day and our living defined by *Your great love for us.* Fill us with holy confidence so that wherever my brothers and sisters are, at work or home or school, Jesus will be glorified in and through us. Do these things, I pray, for the sake of the world around us that is dying without Him.

In the name of Jesus, our Lord and Master. Amen.

Ephesians 3:14-21; Hosea 10:12; Psalm 103:11-12; Acts 17:28; Jeremiah 32:17; Psalm 136

Excelling in the Grace of Giving

But since you excel in everything . . . see that you also excel in
this grace of giving. 2 Corinthians 8:7

Father God, I come before You with praise and thanksgiving in my heart for the great grace and love that You have lavished on me through Christ Jesus. As I have received this day, Lord, may I also freely give to those around me.

I ask also, Father, for my church community (*name of church*), that we, Your people, would become generous in all things.

Pry our fingers off of our possessions that we might increasingly share with those who are in need.

Forgive us for our selfishness with our time and talents, Father. May we turn from self-focused living, generously give of ourselves and engage with the work of Your kingdom.

Remove the fear of "not enough" from our lives, O God! May we joyfully bring our tithes and offerings before You as an act of worship. May we not give out of obligation or reluctantly, but instead, eagerly look for ways to increasingly give more. Help us to deny ourselves.

May those who have never obeyed You in this way be prompted by the Holy Spirit to enter into this discipline of giving back to You. As we do so, Father, throw open heaven and pour out blessing on us that we might be encouraged and our faith strengthened, I pray! *(Pause and pray for your church community, that obedience in regard to the giving of finances, time, and giftings, caring for others—giving in every way—might increase.)*

Forgive us for hoarding and spending our resources without thought of other's needs or expansion of Your kingdom among us. Teach us to lay up treasure in heaven, Lord, for truly, where our treasure is, our hearts will also be engaged. Prompt us by the Holy Spirit that we might set our minds on things unseen and put into action this eternal focus. May we become a community of faith that sows *generously* into Your work, that we might also reap generously.

May we give to You with great joy, a good measure, pressed down, shaken together, and *running over*—that the same might be poured back onto us—and Your kingdom work increase all the more! May we be generous in all things and, in doing so, experience Your great blessing.

For the sake of the world that is still in darkness, use us, Lord, and the resources that You have entrusted to us for everything comes from You, Lord, and belongs to You. *All things are Yours.*

In the name of Jesus, Who became poor that I might be rich, amen.

Ephesians 1:8; 1 John 3:1; Romans 12:13; Matthew 10:8; 2 Corinthians 9:6; Mark 8:34; Malachi 3:10; Matthew 6:20; Luke 12:34, 6:38; Proverbs 22:9; 1 Chronicles 29:14; 2 Corinthians 8:9

Knowing Christ

*I keep asking that the God of our Lord Jesus Christ ... may
give you the Spirit of wisdom and revelation, so that you may
know him better. Ephesians 1:17*

Thank You, Father, for calling me to Yourself and making me Your own through Christ Jesus. This day, I confess and agree with Your Word that everything that I need for life and godliness is found in Him. Forgive me, Lord, for any way in which I have not entered into the deeper life of the Spirit or lived according to Your Word. Through carelessness, I have allowed my faith to become weak and my relationship with Jesus to become distant. In Your great love, restore me, I pray.

I ask also for my brothers and sisters in Christ in my church community, that those who have wandered from the closeness of Your embrace would be brought near once again. Help us to crave spiritual food that we might grow deeper in our relationship with Jesus. May we be mature in our faith, disciplined in training ourselves to distinguish good from evil and feed on the meat of Your Word.

Father, I ask that I and my brothers and sisters in Christ might grow in our knowledge of You. Give us, I pray, a longing to know Christ and the power of His resurrection in our lives. Take us deeper in our walk with You that we may truly become those who have *set our hearts on* pilgrimage with You and be determined to walk with You, to seek and know You. May we grow up in all things through Christ.

To our confession of faith in Him, I ask that goodness be increasingly evident among us, that we might know Christ and make Him known.

To goodness, through revelation by the Holy Spirit through Your Word, add knowledge, I pray, that we might know Christ and make Him known.

To knowledge of You and Your Word, may we grow in self-control in all areas of our living, that we might know Christ and make Him known.

To self-control, I ask that we might be disciplined to persevere in the midst of trials and not lose hope, that we might know Christ and make Him known.

To perseverance, I pray that godliness be added to the core of our being that greater Christlikeness be evident in us, that we might know Him and make Him known.

To godliness, I ask that brotherly kindness be increasingly evident among us through words and actions, that we might know Christ and make Him known.

To brotherly kindness, may we go deeper still and truly love one another. May love increase among us, that we might know Christ more,and make Him known.

Accomplish these things in our faith community (*in me*) I pray, that we might not be ineffective or unproductive, but instead may we grow in grace and knowledge of our Lord and Savior Jesus Christ. Amen and amen.

---

2 Peter 1:3; Psalm 119:9; 1 Peter 2:2; Hebrews 6:1, 5:4; Colossians 1:10, 2:2-3; Ephesians 4:15; Philippians 3:10; Psalm 84:5; 2 Peter 1:5-8, 3:18

Walking in Freedom

It is for freedom that Christ has set us free. Stand firm,
then, and do not let yourselves be burdened again by a yoke
of slavery. Galatians 5:1

Heavenly Father, I praise and thank You that in Christ Your Church has been set free from sin and death! Like the Israelites who You brought out of Egypt, You have broken the bars of our yoke and enabled us to walk with heads held high—Your *sons and daughters*!

I pray today for my brothers and sisters in Christ Jesus, for myself, Lord, that our hearts would become a place where the mystery of the truth that we have been set free from sin can take root, define us and produce change in us. *(Pause and pray for those in your church community whom you know by name.)*

Remove from our lives, I pray, every yoke of slavery. Wake us up to all the ways that we are allowing the enemy to whisper in our ears and define our living by our past instead of the present victory of the cross! Destroy his lies, I pray.

May we increasingly have ears to hear what Your Spirit is saying to us. *(O God, give me ears to hear!)*

May our hearts be defined by the truth of Your Word. *(O God, may the Word be my only standard.)*

May our lives be a consistent expression of walking in the grace, forgiveness, and freedom that we have received. *(May I live a life of love, O God.)*

Set us free from condemnation, I pray! Remove shame, regret, and all evidence of guilt from our lives. Forgive us for living as if we are still slaves to sin. O God, strengthen us to walk in victory. *(Pause and pray for your church community, for your pastor(s), and those you know by name.)*

May my life and the lives of my brothers and sisters be marked by the glorious truth that our sin has been taken away—*wiped from Your memory!* Our debt has been paid! Hallelujah! Infuse our lives, I pray, with great joy in this amazing truth: *Christ Jesus has set us free!*

May we as a faith community be redefined by the work of Christ on our behalf, and may the truth of Your Word renew our minds and thoughts. Strengthen us to turn from self-focused living and fix our eyes on Jesus once again, that we might walk in the freedom He has provided.

I ask this in the name of Jesus, Who came to set captives free. Amen.

Romans 8:2; Leviticus 26:13; 2 Corinthians 6:18; Revelation 2:7; Romans 8:1; Isaiah 43:25, 6:7; Philippians 3:16; Isaiah 61:1

DAY 10

Carrying Each Other's Burdens

Carry each other's burdens, and in this way you will
fulfill the law of Christ. Galatians 6:2

Heavenly Father, I thank You for my brothers and sisters in my church community. Thank You for individual uniqueness and giftings and for the Holy Spirit that unifies us through Christ Jesus. Forgive me, I pray, for I confess that I have not served my brothers and sisters out of love, or considered them better than myself. By the work of the Holy Spirit in me, destroy all self-seeking ways and help me to love Your Church as Jesus does.

Teach us what it means to walk with one another and carry each other's burdens. (*Teach me Lord!*) May each of us be strengthened to bear with the failings of those who are weaker and humbled in order that we might receive encouragement and correction from those who are spiritually stronger. May we put aside our own agendas and opinions, be unified under the banner of Jesus, and love one another deeply from the heart.

I lift before You Father, those in my church community who are weighed down with cares and burdens too great for them to bear. May they be filled with joy and peace and overflow with hope by the power of the Holy Spirit. Give them grace to trust You in all things. (*Pause and pray for those whom the Holy Spirit brings to mind.)*

May we at *(name of church)* become those who reach out to those who are burdened with cares of all kinds or who have fallen away, become discouraged or doubtful in their faith journey. May those who are weak in faith be strengthened and all who stumble be lifted up!

You admonish us in Your Word, Father, that we should gently restore those who are caught in sin. Forgive us, Father, for more often than not we have failed to do this. Keep us from standing in judgment of one another or distancing ourselves from those who are struggling. *(Pause and pray for those in your community of faith who are struggling in their pilgrimage.)*

Teach us by the Holy Spirit within us to be quick to listen, slow to speak, and slow to become angry (or opinionated or preachy). May we increasingly pray together for one another, trusting You in all things. May we truly learn to carry each other's burdens.

Help us this day to walk in love with one another that we might love Your Church as You do, Lord Jesus. I ask these things in Your great name. Amen.

Philippians 2:3-4; 1 Peter 4:8-10; Romans 15:13, 15:1; Galatians 6:1; Ecclesiastes 4:10; Ephesians 4:15; 1 Corinthians 12:26; 2 Timothy 4:2

DAY 11

Praying for Pastors

Quiet your heart before the Lord. Ask for wisdom to know how to pray for your pastor(s). As you pray, insert the name of your pastor(s) into this prayer.

When Moses' hands grew tired, they took a stone and put it under him and he sat on it. Aaron and Hur held his hands up— one on one side, one on the other—so that his hands remained steady till sunset. Exodus 17:12

Heavenly Father, today I come before You with gratitude in my heart for the shepherd that You have placed over my church community. Thank You for our pastor(s). *(Pause before the Lord and give thanks for the shepherd(s) that God has placed over your community of faith.)* As Aaron and Hur held up the arms of Moses, so this day in prayer, I hold up the arms of my pastor that the battle might be won.

I ask Lord, that faith rise up in him that he might trust You more and more for Your work to be accomplished in and through him. May he *overflow with hope* by the power of the Holy Spirit and be encouraged to continue to trust You for the things that he has not yet seen come to pass.

I ask, Father, that You fill my pastor with the knowledge of Your will for our community of faith. Give him spiritual wisdom, insight and understanding. As he studies Your Word, open his mind to ever deeper truths. Renew him by Your Word, I pray.

I ask in Jesus' name that in all things he might be found worthy of his calling and please You in all that he does. By the power of the Holy Spirit, may the work of the ministry—those things prompted by faith—be fulfilled in and through him. May Jesus be glorified through his life and our church community be strengthened by his example.

Lord Jesus Christ, I ask that lasting spiritual fruit be born out of our pastor's life. May the work of his hands be firmly established among us and any weapon of the enemy that has come against him, destroyed in Jesus' name! Give him a sign of your goodness this day, I pray, that those around him will know that Your favor rests on him and may his heart be strengthened in faith.

Strengthen our pastor, Lord, with all power *according to Your great might* at work in him, so that his endurance and patience might increase, for he has devoted himself to Your Church. May we, the Body of Christ called (*name of church community*) follow and respond to our pastor in such a way that his work would be a joy.

In the midst of the burdens that he carries for Your Church, encourage him with joy in the Holy Spirit that he might overflow with thankfulness. May praise and worship be released from his heart as a weapon of warfare, dispelling all unbelief, discouragement, and weariness. Give him new songs to sing, I pray.

This day Lord, be the wall of fire around my pastor, protect him from the evil one and be the glory within him. Awaken his heart with a fresh out pouring of the Holy Spirit, that Your Church might be built up and strengthened through him.

I ask these things in the name of the Great Shepherd, Jesus. Amen.

Exodus 17:12; Romans 15:13; Hebrews 11:1; Colossians 1:9-12; 2 Thessalonians 1:11-12; Psalm 90:17, 86:17; 1 Corinthians 16:15-16; Hebrews 13:17; Numbers 23:20-21; Zechariah 2:5; John 17:15; Hebrews 13:20

DAY 12

Living as Sons and Daughters

So you are no longer a slave, but God's child; and since you
are his child, God has made you also an heir. Galatians 4:7

Heavenly Father, how I thank You for Your provision through Christ to become Your child and for the incredible privilege of belonging to Your family. *(Pause and give thanks for the great gift of salvation.)*

Today, Lord, I come before You on behalf of (*name of your church*) and I ask in the mighty name of Jesus that You reveal to each of us the ways in which we have not yet fully embraced our sonship. You have lavished Your incredible love on us through Christ Jesus, making us Your children, and yet, O God, in so many ways, we continue to live as orphans. Forgive us, I pray.

Help us, Father, to live as *heirs, coheirs* with Christ. By Your Spirit, may this truth land on our hearts and take root! May we walk in this world wearing Your crown of beauty—sons and daughters of the Most High God. Blow away the ash piles of our lives by Your Spirit. Renew us, I pray. *(Pause and pray for your brothers and sisters in Christ Jesus.)*

Heal us from emotional wounds that keep our hearts closed off or distant from You. Tear down the walls of self-protection that we have erected. May the oil of gladness be poured out on my brothers and

31

sisters (on *me*) and mourning and despair be banished from among us. Wrap us in Your garment of praise! *(Ask God for a fresh release of praise and worship to break forth over your church community.)*

Remind us continually, Father, that because of Jesus, we have access to You and can run into Your embrace, crying out "Abba!"—*Daddy*. Call Your Church this day, by the Holy Spirit, into this kind of intimate relationship with You. May my brothers and sisters in Christ in my church family learn to walk, to live—*clothed in Christ*—as those who are heirs to the promise, adopted through Jesus into Your family. *(Pause and pray for those in your church body who may have been wounded by their earthly fathers and ask for healing.)*

This day I ask in Jesus' name that all shame, regret, unworthiness—anything that keeps us from living in the victory of the cross and as Your children—be broken off of the lives of my brothers and sisters *(and my life)*. May we come alive by the Spirit into a fresh realization of what it means to be Yours, turn from "slavery," and walk as Your children, children of the light.

I ask this of You, Father, in the name of my Brother and Savior, Jesus Christ. Amen.

---

1 John 3:1; Romans 8:17; Isaiah 61:3; Hebrews 7:25, 6:19-20, 4:14-16; Galatians 4:6, 3:27-29; 1 Thessalonians 5:5; Matthew 12:50

DAY 13

Continuing in Christ

_So then, just as you received Christ Jesus as Lord, continue
to live your lives in him, rooted and built up in him,
strengthened in the faith as you were taught, and overflowing
with thankfulness. Colossians 2:6-7_

Father, I thank You for my brothers and sisters in Christ Jesus
and the work of Your Spirit among us. Keep changing us, I
pray, that we might more and more become a body of believers who
are determined to be like Jesus.

May we continue to _live in Jesus._ May we truly live and move and
have our very being in Christ alone. Continually remind us that we are
not our own, that we have been bought with a very great price. This
day, may we live in such a way as to bring honor to His name in our
homes, places of work, neighborhoods, and schools. May Jesus be seen
in acts of love and kindness and heard through words of gentleness
and respect through us this day. _(Pause and commit your day, activities,
agendas, and relationships to Christ.)_

May we continue to be _rooted and built up in Christ._ Father, move
us away from the milk of Your Word and increase our hunger to go
deeper. I ask that my brothers and sisters in Christ might truly be like
trees planted by streams of living water, whose roots go down deep,

producing fearless-living regardless of situations and seasons. *(Pause and pray for those whom you know by name.)*

May we continue to be *strengthened in our faith.* May doubt, unbelief, double-mindedness, apathy, and hopelessness be banished from among us. May we once again fix our eyes on Jesus. O God, in Your great mercy, grant us, I pray, eyes that are able to see Your greatness and glory and recognize Your work among us, that our faith might increase.

May we, Your people, *overflow with thankfulness.* In the midst of a complaining culture, may we be those who recognize our many blessings and continually give thanks. Renew our hearts, Father. In the mighty name of the Lord Jesus Christ, may every complaining spirit be banished from among us and may we be *overwhelmed* with joy and thanksgiving. May a river of thankfulness begin to flow from Your Church to the nations of the earth, I pray, in *(name of city in which you live)*, from my community of faith, from *me,* O God. *(Pause and give a thank-offering to the Lord, remembering the many blessings in your life.)*

May my brothers and sisters in Christ be built up this day and the gates of hell not prevail against us—for we are Your Church and it is in Jesus' name and for His glory that I ask these things. Amen.

Acts 17:28; 1 Corinthians 6:19-20; 1 Peter 3:15; Hebrews 5:12-13; Romans 8:29; Jeremiah 17:7-8; Hebrews 12:2; 1 Thessalonians 5:18; Philippians 2:14; Matthew 16:18

Jan 18

Enduring Hardship as Discipline

Endure hardship as discipline; God is treating you as his children. Hebrews 12:7

This day, Father, I come to You asking that You strengthen me and my brothers and sisters in Christ, that we might submit to Your discipline in our lives. Make us mindful, Lord, that the difficulties we face are refining tools in Your hands. Keep us from resisting the work of the Holy Spirit in any way, I pray. Even in the midst of painful circumstances, remind us that You are using all things together for our good, treating us as Your children. *(Pray for those in your church community who are in the midst of trials.)*

Train us in the midst of the trials we face, that a harvest of righteousness and peace might be produced in our lives. May we become more like Jesus!

Give us joy, I pray—unexplainable, overflowing, joy in the Holy Spirit—and remind us that when our faith is tested, perseverance increases. May we remind each other and rejoice together that Jesus has overcome!

Pour out grace on those in our faith community who are suffering. May Your power, Lord Jesus, be made perfect in every weakness.

Teach us to depend on Your strength alone in all things. But for those who cannot endure the trials they are in, I ask for mercy. Provide a way out, I pray.

With the comfort and compassion that we receive from You, may we also comfort others in their troubles. May words of grace, encouragement, and blessing increase in our church community and, may acts of kindness and caring toward those who are suffering multiply.

Use every difficulty that we face to make us strong in You and Your mighty power. May faith rise up in us and increase that we might always stand firm.

Refine the faith of *every* heart, Father, that Jesus might receive praise, glory, and honor in and through us. Strengthen Your church, I pray!

Father, today may we keep our eyes on Jesus and remember what He suffered on our behalf. May it strengthen us so that we will not grow weary or lose heart as we wait on You. In Your great goodness and through all things, teach us Your ways Lord, that we might share in Your holiness and be transformed.

In the name of the Savior, Jesus Christ, who endured the cross. Amen.

Hebrews 12:7-11; Romans 8:28-29; James 1:2-3; John 16:33; 2 Corinthians 12:9; 1 Corinthians 10:13; Ephesians 6:10; 2 Corinthians 1:24; 1 Peter 1:7; 2 Corinthians 1:3; Hebrews 12:2-3

Jan 18

Devoting Ourselves to Prayer

Devote yourselves to prayer, being watchful and thankful.
Colossians 4:2

Father, as I come before You today, I'm so very aware of my own prayerlessness. I think and worry about so much, but pray about so little in comparison. Forgive me, Lord. By the work of the Holy Spirit within me, teach me to pray and to do so continually. *(Be still before the Lord. Pray as the Holy Spirit leads you.)*

I ask also, Lord, for my church community. May my brothers and sisters in Christ be full of joy as they wait on You in the midst of trials that they are experiencing, and may they be faithful in prayer. *(Pray for those in your community of faith who are in difficult circumstances. Ask God to strengthen their faith.)*

Remove from our lives all things that hinder our prayers, unbelief, sin that we have not turned from, unforgiveness and, may we respond to every prompting of the Holy Spirit that we might be unfettered and pray with all of our hearts.

Father, I ask that fervency in prayer and intercession be released on us that we might become a true "house of prayer for all nations." Replace prayerlessness within our fellowship with a passionate longing to see Your Church revived. May prayer become the fuel of the

Holy Spirit among us.

In the name of the Lord Jesus Christ, I ask that we at (*name of church community*) would become those who always pray and never give up. May we be found faithful when You come, Lord Jesus! May we be those that You call upon by the Spirit to watch on the wall for Your Church, for cities and even nations!

I ask that You stir our hearts with an *urgency* to pray and give us full-of-faith, God-sized dreams and requests. Teach us to pray Your heart. Teach us to pray Your Word. May the men of our congregation lead their families on their knees in prayer. May the women of our fellowship humble themselves before You and be self-controlled so that they can pray with greater boldness. Raise up intercessors among the youth of our faith community. Grab hold of their hearts, I pray, and fill them with great faith. May our hearts and minds be set on the things of Your kingdom. Teach us to pray, Lord! From youngest to oldest, teach us to pray!

Do these things I ask so that we, Your Church, might come alive by the Spirit and be allowed the privilege of participating in the harvest that is coming. Even this day, O God, call Your people to humility, to turn from sin, to seek Your face. Wake us up from our slumber, O God, for surely time is short!

In the name of Him who lives to intercede for me, Jesus Christ. Amen.

Luke 11:1; 1 Thessalonians 5:17; Romans 12:12; James 1:6-8; Matthew 6:14-15, 5:23; Psalm 66:18; 1 Peter 3:7; Isaiah 56:7; Mark 11:17; Luke 18:1-8; Isaiah 62:6-7; 1 Peter 4:7; Hebrews 11:13-16; 2 Chronicles 7:14; Romans 13:11-12; Hebrews 7:25

DAY 16

Speaking Truthfully
with One Another

*Therefore each of you must put off falsehood and speak
truthfully to your neighbor, for we are all members of one body.*
Ephesians 4:25

Heavenly Father, I come to You today confessing my great
need of the work of the Holy Spirit in the deepest places of
my heart. It is written in Your Word that You desire truth in my inner
being, so I ask, Father, that truth be found at the core of who I am.

I know the words that I should bring into Your presence, but because
of the falseness of my heart, they so often escape me. O God, have
mercy on me, I pray. Shine the spotlight of the Holy Spirit on every
corner of my heart, expose all darkness and every lie. *(Pause and be
still in God's presence).*

I come to You, Father, on behalf of my church community and ask
that in the hearts of my brothers and sisters in Christ Jesus truth would
also be found. Jesus said that it is out of the overflow of our hearts that
our mouths speak words to build up or tear down. So I ask, Father,
that we might be people of truth deep within our hearts.

May we put off everything that is less than truth, I pray.

Destroy exaggeration, deception of all kinds, false flattery—every expression of falsehood.

May the ways that we lie to protect ourselves, or to avoid admonishing one another be put to death.

Instead, teach us to *speak the truth in love* to one another that we might encourage one another to grow up in Christ and continue in our pilgrimage with Him until we see His face.

In all things, in every opportunity, may we be those who encourage and build each other up as we speak truthfully with one another. Do this, I pray, that Jesus, Who is the Way, the Truth, and the Life, would be seen and proclaimed with greater freedom and joy among us. Begin with me, Lord, for this is the desire of my heart.

I ask this in submission to Your Word, O God, in Jesus' name. Amen.

Psalm 51:6; Isaiah 29:13; Luke 6:45; Colossians 3:9; Ephesians 4:15; Hebrews 10:25; 1 Thessalonians 5:11

Persevering in Doing Good

Let us not become weary in doing good, for at the proper time
we will reap a harvest if we do not give up. Galatians 6:9

Lord Jesus, Your Word admonishes us to not be overcome with evil but to overcome evil with good, and so today I ask that You strengthen my fellowship of believers that we might persevere in doing that which is good. May our gaze be continually on Jesus and all weariness fall away. May the joy of our salvation be our great strength! Increase our "spiritual vision" that we might once again see and understand the privilege of participating with You in Your work. Destroy apathy, laziness, and despair among us. Energize us by Your Spirit.

I pray for my pastor(s) today and ask that You give them a fresh glimpse of the harvest that is coming, that their faith might increase. Firmly establish the work of their hands for Your kingdom among us. Be their burden-bearer today, I pray. (*Pause and pray for your pastor(s) by name.*)

I lift before You those who minister to the children of our fellowship, who teach our youth, who minister on worship teams, who disciple, counsel, and encourage others. O God, may we not grow weary in pointing each other toward Christ! (*Pray for those you know by name who have ministry responsibilities in your church community.*)

May we, as an entire faith community, not grow weary in doing good within the relationships represented among us.

> Strengthen parents to persevere in raising godly children.
> Strengthen husbands and wives to guard their covenant.
> Strengthen those who are single among us to find true community.
> Strengthen our mature saints, that they might continue to proclaim Your great and mighty acts among us with joy and finish well.

Strengthen us, Lord, that we might be known for our good deeds in our neighborhoods, places of work, and schools. May we live in such a way that those around us take note that we belong to Jesus and turn and give You glory.

In all things, Father, at all times and on all occasions, strengthen us to persevere in doing what is good according to Your Word and not give up. May *each of us* be found faithful. Allow us, I pray, the privilege of seeing the harvest come in!

I ask these things in the name of the Lord Jesus Christ. Amen.

Romans 12:21; Hebrews 12:2; Nehemiah 8:10; Psalm 90:17; Matthew 11:30; Psalm 68:19; Proverbs 22:6; Hebrews 13:4; Galatians 5:13; Psalm 71:17-18; Matthew 5:16; Psalm 19:8; Proverbs 6:23; Hebrews 4:12

Worshiping by the Spirit

For [it is] we . . . who worship by the Spirit of God [who]
glory in Christ Jesus. Philippians 3:3 (ESV)

Heavenly Father, it is written that the kind of worshipers You are seeking are those who worship in spirit and in truth. And so this day I come before You, asking for myself and for my church community, that by the presence and power of the Holy Spirit, we might truly worship You with all of our hearts.

Keep us, I pray, from coming before You with only right words. Holy Spirit, awaken our hearts once again that the words of our mouths *and* the depths of our hearts might become one and the same, and be a pleasing sacrifice of truthful worship. May we worship You, Father, for Who You truly are.

Today Lord, I join with Your angels and all Your heavenly hosts and I worship You. I proclaim:

"Holy, holy, holy Lord God Almighty who was and is and
  is to come!
You are worthy to receive glory and honor and power.
For You created all things and by Your will they were created
  and have their being.

To You who sits on the throne and to the Lamb
be praise and honor and glory and power for ever and ever!"

May these worship songs of heaven become the songs of my heart and those of my brothers and sisters in Christ! Open our eyes to the greatness of Your glory. May we be awestruck once again in Your presence. Change us as we worship You. *(Pause and meditate on the greatness, glory, and holiness of our God.)*

Renew us that we might become passionate worshipers, with Spirit-sponsored praise, exalting the Lord Jesus Christ. (*Renew my heart, O Lord!*). May the Holy Spirit be present in power as we gather as a faith community. May He minister in freedom among us, and may our hearts be wide open to His work. May we worship in such a way that the soil of our hearts is prepared to receive the seed of the Word, and the lordship of Jesus is more firmly established in us. *(Pause and pray for your pastor(s) and worship leaders, that they will experience a fresh anointing of the Holy Spirit as they lead His people into His presence.)*

In the name of Jesus, Who is able to keep us from falling into temptation and to present us before Your glorious presence, without fault, to You, the only God our Savior, be glory, majesty, power, and authority, through Jesus Christ our Lord, Who was before the beginning, is now ever-present, and who will soon be here! Hallelujah and AMEN!

John 4:24; Matthew 15:7-9; Psalm 19:14, 103:20-22; Revelation 4:8,11, 5:13; 2 Corinthians 3:17; Luke 8:11-15; Psalm 29:2; 1 Peter 4:11; Jude 25

Discerning What Is Best

And this is my prayer: that your love may abound more and more in knowledge and depth of insight, so that you may be able to discern what is best. Philippians 1:9-10

I praise You, Lord, that everything I need for life and godliness is found in Christ Jesus. Thank You for Your Word and the deposit of the Holy Spirit in my heart that leads me into deeper truth and understanding.

Today, Father, I confess my lack of wisdom. So I ask that You give me Your wisdom. *(Pause and bring before the Lord specific situations you are facing. Ask Him for wisdom for each.)*

For myself and for my church community, I ask that we might be given Your wisdom—wisdom from heaven that is pure, peace loving, considerate, submissive, filled with mercy and good fruit, impartial, and sincere. I pray especially for my brothers and sisters in Christ who are in places of authority in our faith community and ask that they be filled with Your wisdom. *(Pause and pray for pastors, ministry directors, elders, and deacons by name.)*

May we be those who accept Your Words and store them up deep within us. Renew our minds by Your Word.

May we turn toward the deeper things of Your Word, put them

into practice, and be trained by what the Word says! May our ability to discern between good and evil increase.

May we become a faith community that truly hungers for You, Lord, and searches to know and understand You more and more. May wisdom, understanding, and discernment increase among us.

Remove every obstacle that stands in the way of the working of the Holy Spirit in our hearts. May we better comprehend Your Word and gain wisdom and understanding. In Jesus' mighty name, put to death every deceptive philosophy, based on the principles of this world that has taken root in our hearts!

May we, Your people at (*name of church fellowship*), be encouraged in heart by the Holy Spirit and unified in our love for You so that we might enter into greater understanding of the mystery of Christ. This day I confess that in Him alone are hidden all the treasures of wisdom and knowledge. In knowing You, Lord, we truly know what is best. May our hearts truly be set on pilgrimage with You this day. Take us deeper, Lord. Take us deeper still.

In Your name alone, Jesus. Amen.

---

2 Peter 1:3; 2 Corinthians 1:22; James 1:5-8, 3:17; Romans 12:1-2; Proverbs 2:1-6; Hebrews 5:14; 1 Corinthians 2:10,12,15; Colossians 2:8, 2:2-3; Psalm 84:5

Experiencing the Fullness of Christ

For in Christ all the fullness of the Deity lives in bodily form,
and in Christ you have been brought to fullness.
Colossians 2:9-10

Heavenly Father, as I quiet myself before You and begin to contemplate that I have been given Your fullness through Christ, I confess that I cannot begin to grasp what this means or how it can possibly be displayed in my life. Open my spiritual eyes and understanding, I pray, that what I know to be true—that I can be filled to the measure of all Your fullness—might become a reality in the way I live. *(Pause and ask the Lord for a fresh infilling of the Holy Spirit and insight, understanding, and strength that you might appropriate what God has provided through Christ.)*

I bring before You my church community *(pray for by name)* and I ask, Lord, that each of us might experience Your fullness in our lives in greater measure. May we *overflow* with Jesus!

May we put to death all deeds of darkness, exposing them to the light of Your presence through brokenness and repentance. May the fruit of the light—goodness, righteousness, and truth—increase in our lives. May our living be motivated by our great love for You. May we be diligent in making room for Your greater fullness. *(Pause and ask that godly sorrow, that brings true repentance, might be given to you and your faith community.)*

Unify us in our faith in You and the truth that we know of Jesus Christ. May we receive the Word as we should—not as words of men, but as it actually is—*Your very Word!* Do this, I pray, that we might grow up in You and attain the whole measure of the fullness of Christ Jesus.

I lift up before You, our pastor(s). Fill them, I pray, with the full measure of the fullness of Christ. May Jesus be seen in them and His love expressed through them with greater and greater fervency. *(Pause and pray for your pastor(s) by name.)*

Our elders and deacons, those who teach, disciple, and counsel— may they be filled to overflowing with Jesus. *(Pause and pray for those you know by name.)*

From youngest to oldest, O God, may we become a community of faith that is filled up with Christ Jesus. May we be found steadfast in Him, and truly know Him and the power of His resurrection in our lives in such a way that we are strengthened to enter into the fellowship of His sufferings.

Jesus, fill us up with more of Yourself, pushing out all that is not conformed to Your image, that we might overflow with Your likeness. Accomplish this in us through presence and power of the Holy Spirit. I ask this in Your name, Lord Jesus, for in You alone is the fullness of life. Amen.

Ephesians 3:19, 5:8-12; Colossians 2:2-3; Philippians 3:16; 2 Corinthians 7:10; 1 Thessalonians 2:12-13; Ephesians 4:13; Philippians 3:8-10; Romans 8:29

Keeping in Step with the Spirit

Since we live by the Spirit, let us keep in step with the Spirit.
Galatians 5:25

Heavenly Father, I thank You for the gift of the Holy Spirit as a deposit in my heart, confirming that through Jesus, I have been adopted into Your family. Thank You for the ministry of the Holy Spirit in my heart and life and the lives of those in my church community.

Give us, I pray, a willingness of heart to submit to the leading and promptings of the Holy Spirit as He guides us into deeper truth. May we not resist the Holy Spirit in any way or ignore or make excuses for sin in our lives. Forgive us for going our own way, for doing our own thing, for shutting our ears to Your voice. In Your kindness, draw us to repentance. *(Pause and pray for your community of faith, that the work of the Holy Spirit will increase in each life, producing holiness. Ask God to give your church community the gift of repentance.)*

Teach us, I pray, what it means to "walk in the Spirit" and "keep in step with the Spirit" in our everyday, moment-by-moment living, that we would increasingly be those who do not gratify the desires of the sinful nature. Father, I ask in the mighty name of Jesus that the passions of our sinful natures *be put to death so* that the fruit of the Spirit might increase in our lives.

May love and joy be expressed with increasing measure among us. May we truly love what You love, Father, and be filled with the joy of our salvation!

May the peace of Christ expressed through the unity of the Spirit, and enduring patience with one another be evident in our relationships.

May genuine acts and words of kindness and goodness increase in our fellowship. May we consider one another's needs as more important than our own.

May faithfulness and gentleness in our relationships with one another be evident at all times.

May we embrace a lifestyle of denying ourselves and taking up our crosses and following You Lord Jesus, choosing to be self-controlled in all things.

(Pause and pray for your church community, asking that the fruit of the Spirit might be increasingly seen in your life and the lives of your brothers and sisters.)

Lord Jesus, this day I confess that apart from You, I can do nothing. My brothers and sisters can do nothing. And so I ask, strengthen us to abide in You. Call us continually to "vine and branch" living, connected to You in all things at all times. Do this, I pray, that we might produce the fruit of the Spirit in our lives and walk as children of the light. In Your mighty name, I pray these things. Amen.

---

2 Corinthians 1:22; John 16:13; Psalm 51:12; Romans 2:4; Galatians 5:16-18, 22-23; Philippians 2:3-4; Mark 8:34; John 15:4-5; Ephesians 5:8

Expressing Faith through Love

*The only thing that counts is faith expressing itself
through love. Galatians 5:6*

Father, I thank You for Your Word and the theme of love,
mercy, and forgiveness that is woven throughout its pages.
Thank You, Lord Jesus, for Your ultimate example and expression of
love in dying for me—the Righteous for the unrighteous—that I might
be brought into the family of God. Holy Spirit, fill me with the love
and compassion of Christ, I pray. *(Pause and give thanks for the love of
Jesus expressed through the cross. Ask for a fresh infilling of the Holy Spirit.)*

Forgive me, Father, for any way that I have harbored bitterness,
unforgiveness, prejudice, or a judgmental spirit against brothers and
sisters in Christ. *(Pause and pray for those whom the Holy Spirit brings
to mind. Choose to forgive them in Christ.)*

May my life and those in my church community be marked by love
and forgiveness, Father, and may it begin with me. May we forgive others
as we have been forgiven and do so deeply from the heart. *(Pause and
pray that love and forgiveness might increase in your faith community.)*

Father, Your Word says: "If anyone says, 'I love God,' yet hates his
brother, he is a liar; for he who does not love his brother whom he has
seen, how can he love God, whom he has not seen?" (NKJV). Remove

insincerity, hatred, envy, and discord of all kinds, and replace all hatred and anger with the love and compassion of Christ!

It is written: Love "always protects, always trusts, always hopes, always perseveres." Teach Your Church to love, O God.

It is written: "By this everyone will know that You are my disciples, if you love one another." Teach us this way of living out the gospel.

In Jesus' mighty name, may we truly serve one another in love—each of us loving others as we love ourselves—and in so doing be strengthened in faith to do the same in the marketplaces of our lives. May our actions increasingly line up with the truth that we confess with our mouths. In all things, may we follow Your example, Lord Jesus, and walk as You walked, loving as You loved.

O loving Savior, I ask these things in Your name. Amen.

Psalm 86:5; 1 Peter 3:18; Colossians 3:13; Matthew 6:14-15; 1 John 4:20; 1 Corinthians 13:7; John 13:35; Galatians 5:13-14

DAY 23

Striving as One for the Faith

*I will know that you stand firm in one Spirit, striving
together as one for the faith of the gospel. Philippians 1:27*

Heavenly Father, this day I declare over my life and my church
community that the gospel of Jesus Christ is *good news*. Our
sins have been forgiven *(Thank You Lord!)*. Our debt has been paid in
full *(Hallelujah!)*. There is no record held against us! I confess that this
great salvation is found only in You, Lord Jesus Christ. There is no
other name by which men must be saved.

I ask that the Holy Spirit be poured out on us, Lord, filling us with
awe and wonder once again at this great gift of salvation. Forgive us,
Father, for the ways that we live as if we are ashamed of the gospel of
Christ. Remove timidity from our lives and every fear that holds us
back from living out our faith in love.

Make us ready, Lord, to give the reason for the hope that we have.
May we live in such a way that those around us will notice that we
belong to Jesus. May our words be filled with gentleness and respect.
*(Pray for those whom God has placed in your life who do not yet know
Him. Pray that you will represent Christ before them as you should.)*

May we turn from human wisdom and increasingly be people of
Your Word in all that we do and say, that our gospel witness might not

be emptied of its power. Help us, Lord, to live in such a way that we are worthy of You and Your calling on our lives.

Because we have put our hope in You, O Lord—the living God who is the Savior of all men—may we labor and strive together that many might come to know Jesus. Father, give us spiritual harvest, I pray!

I ask that all that we do as a church community be an expression of faith and love. May our lives be marked by great endurance that is inspired by our hope in Jesus Christ. Strengthen us, Lord (strengthen *me*) with hope through the Holy Spirit that we might not grow weary but see the harvest come in.

This day, Lord, may our faith—the good news in Jesus Christ—be lived out through my life and the lives of my brothers and sisters in Christ, not just with words, but power and the Holy Spirit and deep conviction. Do this, I pray, that the world may know that we are Yours, and would long to know You.

In the name of my Savior and Master, Jesus. Amen.

Colossians 2:13-14; Psalm 103:12; Acts 4:12; Romans 1:16; 2 Timothy 1:7; 1 Peter 3:15; 1 Corinthians 1:17; I Thessalonians 2:12; 1 Timothy 4:10; 1 Thessalonians 1:3; Romans 15:13; Galatians 6:9; 1 Thessalonians 1:5

Doing Everything in the Strength of Christ

I can do all things through Christ who strengthens me.
Philippians 4:13 (NKJV)

Lord Jesus Christ, this day I confess that You are the True Vine and we, Your people, are Your branches. I ask that I and my brothers and sisters might be reminded continually that unless we are connected to You, there will be no lasting spiritual fruit produced by our lives. May we respond to Your voice calling us into deeper intimacy with You. Teach us to *abide* in Your presence. *(Pause and pray for those in your church community that they will listen for and respond to the Holy Spirit. Ask that your ears might be tuned to His voice.)*

May we, Your Church, be strengthened with the resurrection power of Christ so that we might be able to turn back the battles of our lives and stand firm in our faith. For we can do all things through Christ who gives us strength. *(Pray for those in your community of faith who are experiencing trials. Ask that they might be strengthened to persevere.)*

Strengthen our hearts, I pray, that we might live our lives in such a way that we will be found blameless and holy in Your presence when You return, Lord Jesus. For it is Your will that we should be holy and live lives that are pleasing to You. Strengthen us with power through the Holy Spirit, I pray, for without You we can do nothing. *(Pray that a greater hunger for holiness will be poured out on your church community.)*

Build Your Church through us, Father; we do not want to labor in vain! Keep us from serving, ministering, *living* in our own strength. Forgive us for the ways that we have relied on our own wisdom, abilities, and resources instead of Your Spirit. May we serve and minister with hearts that are fully devoted to You, and be strengthened, for without You we can do nothing. *(Pray for the ministries of your faith community asking that those who serve will minister in the strength of Christ through the power of the Holy Spirit. Pray for your pastor(s).)*

I ask that we be reminded continually by the Holy Spirit that it is Christ in us, the hope of glory, who strengthens us to fearlessly engage in the work of the kingdom in all we do. This day, Father, may our lives be marked by increasing boldness, confidence—even risk taking—for the sake of Your Church and a world that does not yet know You. May You be strong in and through us. Your mighty power displayed and Your name glorified. For we can do all things through You, Lord Jesus, Who gives us strength.

Be our strength this day, I ask in Your name. Amen.

John 15:5; Ephesians 1:19-20; Isaiah 28:6; 2 Chronicles 20:12; 1 Thessalonians 3:13, 4:3,7; Ephesians 3:16; Psalm 127:1; Zechariah 4:6; Isaiah 31:1; Colossians 1:27; Matthew 11:12; Ephesians 6:10

Sharing in the Authority of Christ

And God raised us up with Christ and seated us with him in the heavenly realms in Christ Jesus. Ephesians 2:6

Lord Jesus, I thank You for resurrection power that is available to Your Church because of Your finished work on the cross and Your victory over death and the grave. Thank You for the forgiveness of sins, for disarming the powers of darkness and triumphing over them by the cross! You are Head over every power and authority, with all things under Your feet.

This day, Father, I ask for greater understanding of the truths that I share in the authority of Christ and that I have been given all fullness in Him and through Him. I ask this for myself, Lord, for my brothers and sisters in Christ at (*name of church*) and for Your Church around the world. By the presence of the Holy Spirit in us, may we move from merely pronouncing this Truth with our mouths, to deep heart-belief that defines the way we live.

Remind us continually that because of the loving sacrifice of Jesus, we are *more than* conquerors. May faith rise up in our hearts regardless of what we can see with our eyes.

Give us greater hunger for Your Word that our knowledge of You might increase and Your divine power be lived out through us, producing life and godliness.

May we turn from fear and timidity and be strong in You and in Your mighty power.

Forgive us, Father, for the ways that we act as if we are victims of sin. Destroy the excuses that we make for thoughts, words, and actions that are contrary to Your Word. Wake us up from our slumber! May we put aside all deeds of darkness, taking authority in Jesus' mighty name, and put on the armor of light! May we be clothed in Christ.

(Pause and pray for your church community. Ask God for a fresh out-pouring of the Holy Spirit that opens spiritual eyes to see the true condition of our hearts and understand the blessings that are ours in Christ.)

Lord Jesus Christ, You have declared that You will build Your Church and that the gates of hell will not prevail against it. Build *me* today, Lord! Build up my brothers and sisters in Christ! Remind Your Church that the victory is ours through Jesus and that our true struggle is not against what we can see, but against the enemy of our souls.

I ask these things in the authority of the mighty name of the Lord Jesus Christ, Who rules over all. Amen and AMEN.

Colossians 2:13-15; 1 Corinthians 15:17,20; Colossians 2:9; Romans 8:37; Hebrews 11:1; Isaiah 29:13; 2 Peter 1:3-4; 2 Timothy 1:7; Ephesians 6:10; Romans 13:11-14; Matthew 16:18; 1 Corinthians 15:57-58; Ephesians 6:12

Dwelling on What Is Excellent

If anything is excellent or praiseworthy—think about
such things. Philippians 4:8

Heavenly Father, I come before You in the name of Jesus for myself and on behalf of my brothers and sisters in Christ. I ask that this day we might be strengthened by the Holy Spirit to take every thought captive and make it obedient to Jesus! May our relationships, our service and ministries, our worship, conversations, and daily living be *transformed by the renewing of our minds.*

May all unwholesome, ungodly thoughts—things that are contrary to the standard of Your Word and not like Jesus—be put to death in us. May we once again guard our hearts above all else, knowing that what we feed our minds fuels our attitudes and words. *(Pause and be still before the Lord. Ask the Holy Spirit to reveal to you in what way you have allowed the enemy to influence your thinking.)*

Forgive us, Father, for we have not disciplined our minds. We have given into the patterns of the world, entertained ourselves with things based on the principles of this world and allowed our minds to become numb. We have not nurtured the mind of Christ.

Father, I ask that we would increasingly be a community of faith that hungers earnestly for Your Word. May we not resist the ways that it judges our thoughts and attitudes but live in submission to the truth—agreeing with Your Word and putting it into practice. Wash our minds with the Word, I pray.

I ask, Lord Jesus, that this day, we Your Church, would engage the battle for our minds. May the words of our mouths *and the meditations of our hearts* truly be pleasing to You. May our minds be controlled by the Holy Spirit, so that life and peace might flow from our lives!

By the work of the Holy Spirit in each of us, Lord, begin to change our faith community from the inside out this day. Wake us up to the ways that we are giving into the evil one in our thinking. May our hearts and minds be filled with the truth of Your Word, prayer, and blessing and our lives overflow with noble, right, and pure living.

Do this Lord Jesus, that Your Church might come alive and that You might receive the glory due Your name in and through us. Amen.

---

2 Corinthians 10:5; Romans 12:2; Proverbs 4:23; Luke 6:45; Colossians 2:8; 1 Corinthians 2:16; Hebrews 4:12; James 1:22; Psalm 19:14; Romans 8:6; Philippians 4:8

Wrestling in Prayer

. . . always wrestling in prayer for you, that you may stand
firm in all the will of God, mature and fully assured.
Colossians 4:12

Heavenly Father, it is in the name of the Lord Jesus Christ that I come before You. Because of His shed blood on the cross and His triumph over spiritual powers and authorities, I take my stand in His authority, through prayer, against the schemes of the evil one that are against my church community.

This day, I declare that Jesus is the Christ, the Son of the Living God—that there is salvation in no other name. Jesus is *the* Way, *the* Truth and *the* Life—no one comes to You, Father, except through Him! May this declaration rise up in the hearts of Your people and be foundational to the building of Your church. *(Pray for your faith community by name that deeper faith in and submission to the lordship of Jesus would emerge and strengthen every heart.)*

I acknowledge, Father, that the battles that we face as Your Church are not against what we can see, but against what is unseen in heavenly places. This day, through prayer, I raise the banner of Jesus over my church community. I ask that all strongholds, arguments, and everything at work among us—all that sets itself up against Your people truly knowing You, O God—*be demolished*! Strengthen us to stand firm in our faith.

May the words of our faith journey, our testimony of who Jesus is to us, be rooted in our hearts and spoken of freely, that we might truly be overcomers. May faith rise up in us. Give us victory, I pray!

Open our eyes once again that we might be aware that the enemy of our souls is always on the prowl, looking for opportunity to destroy Your work among us and in us. Remind us that Christ in us is greater than the enemy of our souls!

I ask in the mighty name of the Lord Jesus Christ that spiritual gates be opened in heavenly places on behalf of my church community. May we pass through and into the next thing that You have for us!

In prayer, I prepare the way for Your people, O God. May we not resist Your leading in the way that we should go. May the pathways into our hearts be broadened and made smooth by the Holy Spirit.

Father, remove all obstacles from our lives, every stone. Fill every pothole. Rebuild us in all things and in every way where we have allowed the condition of our hearts—and therefore Your Church—to fall into disrepair. *(Be still before the Lord. Pray as the Holy Spirit directs you.)*

May the banner of Jesus be seen and proclaimed over our lives and every weapon of the evil one that has been forged against us be destroyed. Build Your Church, Lord, and may the gates of hell not prevail against us—for *we are Yours!*

In the name of the Lord Jesus Christ Who is Head of the Church, may it be so. Amen and Amen!

---

2 Corinthians 10:3-5; Matthew 16:16-18; Acts 4:12; John 14:6; Ephesians 6:12; Psalm 60:4; Isaiah 7:9; Revelation 12:11; 1 John 5:4; 1 Peter 5:8; John 10:10; 1 John 4:4; Isaiah 62:10; Proverbs 16:17; Isaiah 54:17; Psalm 95:7

Putting Off the Old Self

You were taught, with regard to your former way of life,
to put off your old self, which is being corrupted by its
deceitful desires. Ephesians 4:22

Here I am, Lord, aware of my great need of You and the places of my heart yet in need of Your healing and renewing touch. *(Be still before the Lord. Acknowledge that He is God. Ask Him to change you from the inside out.)*

Thank You, Lord Jesus, for taking my sins upon Yourself on the cross—for paying my debt. Strengthen me with the power of the Holy Spirit, that I might truly die to the influence of sin in my life and live a lifestyle that pursues righteousness.

I pray this also for my church community, that we would truly put to death everything that belongs to our earthly nature. May sexual immorality, impurity, lust of all kind, evil desires and greed be eradicated from among us by the Holy Spirit. May we truly become alive in You!

I ask that You open our spiritual eyes that we might be aware of:

the ways that the enemy of our souls has taken us captive,

where we have allowed sin to grow and take root,

where we are making excuses for thoughts, emotions, and

behavior that are contrary to Your Word.
every way and area of our lives where the "old self" is still
reigning

Your Word admonishes us to live in this world as those who do not belong. Teach us, Holy Spirit, how to love others and engage people as Jesus did and yet live as an "alien and stranger." May we not love the world or the things that it represents. Instead, may our faith community be marked by a holy determination to throw off everything in our lives that trips us up or slows us down in our following after You, Lord Jesus. May sin not rule over us.

Thank You for setting us free, Lord Jesus! Forgive us for the ways that we return to a yoke of slavery and nurture our old selves. Strengthen us to stand firm in the victory of the cross.

May we this day crucify our sinful nature and walk in the truth of Your Word. *(Pause and pray for your brothers and sisters in Christ whom you know by name. Ask God to strengthen them by the Holy Spirit to walk worthy of their calling in Christ.)*

In the name of Jesus who has conquered sin. Amen.

Psalm 46:10; 1 Peter 2:24; Colossians 3:5; Romans 6:11; 1 Peter 2:11; 1 John 2:15-17; Hebrews 12:1; Romans 6:14; Galatians 5:1; Ephesians 4:1

Forgetting What Is Behind

*But one thing I do: Forgetting what is behind and straining
toward what is ahead . . . Philippians 3:13*

Heavenly Father, I thank You that in Christ, I have been made new. Jesus has taken my punishment upon Himself and the blanket of sin that shrouded my life is gone! Hallelujah! Thank You, Father, that there is no condemnation, nothing held against me. You have wiped my record clean with the blood of the Lord Jesus Christ! *(Pause and give a thank-offering to the Lord for this great salvation!)*

I ask, Lord, in light of this great truth, that we, Your people, be strengthened and reminded by the Holy Spirit to forget the former things and stop dwelling on the past. I ask for my brothers and sisters in Christ in my church community that You blow away the ash piles of our lives by the Holy Spirit. Where there is mourning or despair, pour out Your gladness and robe us in praise. Bind up the brokenhearted and wounded among us, Lord, for in Christ Jesus, there is healing and freedom! *(Pause and pray for those in your faith community by name, asking for greater freedom and victory over past sin and hurt.)*

I ask, Father, that as a church community we might become more determined to throw off everything that hinders the effectiveness of our race of faith—including the ways that we have allowed our living to be defined by past sin, brokenness, and hurt.

Teach us to walk in victory as *more than* conquerors through Christ—living up to what we have already received through Him!

May our minds be renewed by Your Word and our living transformed. Destroy every way in which we are still bound to our past. Break the chains, Lord! May we see ourselves as You do, O God, wearing the righteousness of Christ!

This day, Lord, I ask that You fill Your Church with a fresh determination to move forward in our journey with You. Strengthen us to persevere with joy and to be disciplined, that we might push forward into the next thing that You have for us. Like the Apostle Paul, may we truly *press on*!

Do this, I pray, that this great salvation that is ours might define everything about who we are and empower us to live boldly for our Savior.

In the name of Jesus, Who alone is worthy. Amen.

---

2 Corinthians 5:17; Isaiah 25:7-8; Romans 8:1; 1 John 1:7; Isaiah 43:18, 61:1-3; Hebrews 12:1-2; Romans 8:37; Philippians 3:16; Romans 12:1-2; Psalm 147:3; 2 Corinthians 5:21; Isaiah 43:19; Philippians 3:13-14

Proclaiming the Greatness of Our God

I will come and proclaim your mighty acts, . . . I will proclaim your righteous deeds, yours alone. Psalm 71:16

How blessed we are, Father, that You are our God—that because of Jesus, we belong to You! We are Your people, the sheep of Your pasture the flock under Your care. *(Pause and praise God that He has called you to Himself.)*

Today, Father, I agree with Your Word, and I confess that it is You who has taught us and led us. It is Your faithful love that has sustained us! Now Lord, open our mouths and release our lips that we might become a church community that declares Your power and might to the next generation—for You have done great things and there is none like You!

May our joyful proclamation continually be that You are great and worthy of our praise! Through us Lord, receive the glory that is due Your name.

May we recount the stories of the mighty things that You have done, telling and proclaiming the miraculous ways that You have intervened and provided for us!

May "stones of remembrance" be shared among our faith community—testimonies of Your faithfulness—for more times than we can recount, You have parted the waters before us and made a way where there was none.

This day, Father, may we as the church community called (name of church) remember and proclaim Your mighty power expressed in our lives. May the stories of our hearts be dusted off and spoken of once again for You, O God:

> have provided in famine. *(Pause and remember the provision of God for your needs and give thanks.)*
> have delivered from death. *(Pause and remember God's intervention in your life situations and give thanks.)*
> have set captives free. *(Pause and remember when you were in darkness and what it means that you are now a child of the Light, and give thanks.)*
> restores what has been stolen. *(Pause and give thanks for His redeeming grace and power in your life.)*

Increase our boldness in proclaiming Your greatness, Father, that our children and youth will be encouraged to follow You whole heartedly and become proclaimers of Your greatness and goodness as well!

Release joyful proclamation over my brothers and sisters in Christ Jesus this day, Lord, that we might give You the glory due Your name! (Pray for those in your community of faith that you know by name.) May the overflow of our hearts be heard again and again through stories of Your greatness, goodness, provision and saving power in our lives. For truly You have done amazing things, Lord, and You are worthy of all our praise! To You alone be all Glory! Hallelujah and Amen.

Psalm 79:13, 95:7, 136:1-4, 71:16-19, 119:171; Psalm 145; Joshua 4:4-7; Philippians 4:19; Psalm 34:7; Isaiah 61:1; Joel 2:25; Romans 8:28; 1 Chronicles 16:29

Awaiting the Savior

*But our citizenship is in heaven. And we eagerly await a
Savior from there, the Lord Jesus Christ. Philippians 3:20*

How grateful I am this day, Father, for the promise of Jesus'
return. Make my heart ready, Lord, that I might watch and
wait with great faith and eagerness in my heart.

For my church community as well, I ask that You strengthen each
and every one of us to say "no" to ungodliness and the passions of
this world. May we be self-controlled, upright, and godly in all that
we do as we wait for Jesus, our *blessed hope*, in order that we might
be confident and unashamed before Him when He comes. *(Pause
and pray for your faith community. Pray that all doubt and unbelief
regarding the Second Coming of Christ be destroyed and replaced with
holy anticipation.)*

Forgive us, Father, for the ways that we have allowed ourselves to
become entangled with the things of this world. We have allowed our
hearts to be weighed down with the anxieties of life, and, in so doing,
our watchfulness for the coming of Jesus has been diminished! Awaken
our hearts, I pray!

Instead of setting our minds on things above, our thoughts have
become cluttered with the passing affairs of this world. We have not

been clear-minded so that we can pray. Forgive us, Father, and heal Your Church.

We have become inattentive to Your work and weary as we wait. O Lord, have mercy on us. Revive our hearts once again and give us a fresh sense of urgency that produces greater love and devotion and a living out of our faith. May we be patient and stand firm as we wait, for surely Your coming is near, Lord Jesus!

I ask, Lord Jesus, that when You return, You will find me and my brothers and sisters in Christ dressed and ready for service with our lamps fully fueled and burning brightly. May we truly live as aliens and strangers in this world, ministering the love of Christ in word and deed.

Lord Jesus, may we be always watching for Your return and encouraging each other continually that *today could be the day*!

Maranatha! O Lord Jesus, come quickly, I pray! Amen and AMEN!

Titus 2:12-13; 1 John 2:28; Luke 21:34; Psalm 73:25; Colossians 3:2; 1 Peter 4:7; James 5:8; 1 Peter 2:11; Luke 12:35-40

Praying for My Church Community Journal

Use the following pages to organize your ongoing prayers for your church. There are sections to pray for pastors, church leaders, ministries, and specific people.

We encourage you to keep this close to your Bible. Use the blank spaces to write down verses or scripture promises the Lord gives you as you pray. Jot down the page numbers of the specific prayers from this book that you pray over these individuals and ministries. Make sure you read the Scriptures at the bottom of each prayer as a starting point to further prayer.

PRAYING FOR THOSE IN
SPIRITUAL AUTHORITY

We constantly pray for you, that our God may make you worthy of his calling, and that by his power he may bring to fruition your every desire for goodness and your every deed prompted by faith. 2 Thessalonians 1:11

PASTOR(S) *(list by name)*

PRAYING FOR THOSE IN SPIRITUAL AUTHORITY

Prayer Prompters and Scripture Promises

PRAYING FOR THOSE IN
SPIRITUAL AUTHORITY

Now the overseer is to be above reproach . . . They must keep
hold of the deep truths of the faith with a clear conscience.
1 Timothy 3:2,9

ELDERS (*list by name*)

DEACONS (*list by name*)

PRAYING FOR THOSE IN SPIRITUAL AUTHORITY

COUNCIL & GOVERNING MEMBERS (*list by name*)

Prayer Prompters and Scripture Promises

PRAYING FOR THE MINISTRIES OF MY CHURCH COMMUNITY

. . . stand firm. Let nothing move you. Always give yourselves fully to the work of the Lord, because you know that your labor in the Lord is not in vain. 1 Corinthians 15:58

CHRISTIAN EDUCATION, DISCIPLESHIP, & TEACHING

Prayer Prompters and Scripture Promises

PRAYING FOR THE MINISTRIES OF MY CHURCH COMMUNITY

CHRISTIAN EDUCATION, DISCIPLESHIP, & TEACHING

Prayer Prompters and Scripture Promises

PRAYING FOR THE MINISTRIES OF
MY CHURCH COMMUNITY

MISSION AND OUTREACH

Prayer Prompters and Scripture Promises

PRAYING FOR THE MINISTRIES OF
MY CHURCH COMMUNITY

MISSION AND OUTREACH

Prayer Prompters and Scripture Promises

PRAYING FOR THE MINISTRIES OF MY CHURCH COMMUNITY

PRAYER & COUNSELING

Prayer Prompters and Scripture Promises

PRAYING FOR THE MINISTRIES OF
MY CHURCH COMMUNITY

PRAYER & COUNSELING

Prayer Prompters and Scripture Promises

PRAYING FOR THE MINISTRIES OF
MY CHURCH COMMUNITY

CELL & SMALL GROUPS

Prayer Prompters and Scripture Promises

PRAYING FOR THE MINISTRIES OF
MY CHURCH COMMUNITY

CELL & SMALL GROUPS

Prayer Prompters and Scripture Promises

PRAYING FOR THE NEXT GENERATION

*My prayer is not that you take them out of the world but that
you protect them from the evil one. John 17:15
But grow in the grace and knowledge of our Lord and Savior
Jesus Christ. To him be glory both now and forever! Amen.
2 Peter 3:18*

CHILDREN (*list by name*)

Prayer Prompters and Scripture Promises

PRAYING FOR THE NEXT GENERATION

YOUTH (*list by name*)

Prayer Prompters and Scripture Promises

PRAYING FOR THE NEXT GENERATION

YOUNG ADULTS (*list by name*)

Prayer Prompters and Scripture Promises

PRAYING FOR THE NEXT GENERATION

Prayer Prompters and Scripture Promises

PRAYING FOR FAMILIES IN MY CHURCH COMMUNITY

Wives, submit to your own husbands as you do to the Lord. . . .
Husbands, love your wives, just as Christ loved the church and
gave himself up for her. Children . . . honor your father and
mother . . . Fathers, do not exasperate your children; instead,
bring them up in the training and instruction of the Lord.
Ephesians 5:22-6:4

COVENANT MARRIAGE RELATIONSHIPS (*list by name*)

Prayer Prompters and Scripture Promises

PRAYING FOR FAMILIES IN MY CHURCH COMMUNITY

PARENT-CHILD RELATIONSHIPS *(list by name)*

Prayer Prompters and Scripture Promises

PRAYING FOR FAMILIES IN MY CHURCH COMMUNITY

SINGLE PARENTS *(list by name)*

Prayer Prompters and Scripture Promises

PRAYING FOR FAMILIES IN MY CHURCH COMMUNITY

PRODIGAL CHILDREN (*list by name*)

Prayer Prompters and Scripture Promises

PRAYING FOR FAMILIES IN MY CHURCH COMMUNITY

THOSE WHO WAIT THEIR RETURN (*list by name*)

Prayer Prompters and Scripture Promises

Stay Connected

with

If you were blessed by these prayers, we invite you to connect with Pray the Word through our website and social network pages.

praytheword.net

- Find additional prayers to download--in multiple languages.
- Find other helps to encourage you in your desire to pray the Word.
- Sign up for updates on resources.

Connect with Us on Facebook
facebook.com/praytheword

- Be reminded regularly to pray the Word.
- Interact with others who are praying the Word.
- Be the first to know of new prayers that are available
- Post your own scripture-based prayers

Pray the Word is sponsored by Harvest Prayer Ministries (harvestprayer.com).

RESOURCES
Available from Pray the Word

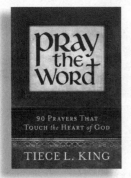

Pray the Word:
90 Prayers That Touch the Heart of God

Includes 90 powerful prayers that can move your prayer life from a fix-it focus to one that desires and surrenders to the purposes of God. Each prayer also includes space to journal either what God is saying to you or to write out additional requests the prayers stimulate in you. (Note: The first 30 prayers in this book are also included in *Pray the Word: 31 Prayers That Touch the Heart of God*.)

Available from your local Christian bookstore and prayershop.org.

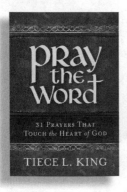

Pray the Word:
31 Prayers That Touch the Heart of God

Includes a month of scripture-based prayers that will take your prayer life to a deeper level. These prayers are not focused on our daily needs or problems, but will move us to surrender to the desires the Father has for us.

Available from your local Christian bookstore and prayershop.org.

If purchasing a quantity for your friends or church, go to prayershop.org, which has deep discounts on multiple copies.

Get the *Pray the Word* App

One month of *Pray the Word* is available as a free App for Apple and Android smartphones. The prayers are available in English, Spanish, Chinese, Indonesian, Thai, and Japanese with more languages being added as they become available. Enjoy the convenience of praying whenever you felt led to do so.

Go to the App store on your phone and search for "Pray the Word."

Get Your Congregation Praying!

You have enjoyed praying through *Pray the Word for Your Church*. Imagine what impact an entire congregation praying out of *Pray the Word for Your Church* might have on your fellowship! Let this resource stimulate a passion in your people to pray for your church.

PrayerShop has discounts on multiple copies, starting with as few as five copies. Go to prayershop.org to see the discounts and place your order. Or if you want to support a local Christian bookstore, have it contact us. We will give them a greater discount so they can order the books for you.

800-217-5200 | 812-238-5504
www.prayershop.org

PRAYERSHOP
PUBLISHING

PRAYERCONNECT

Connecting to the Heart of Christ through Prayer

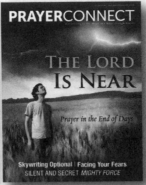
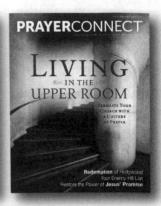

A NEW BIMONTHLY MAGAZINE DESIGNED TO:

Equip prayer leaders and pastors with tools to disciple their congregations.

Connect intercessors with the growing worldwide prayer movement.

Mobilize believers to pray God's purposes for their church, city and the nations.

Each issue of *Prayer Connect* includes:
- Practical articles to equip and inspire your prayer life.
- Helpful prayer tips and proven ideas.
- News of prayer movements around the world.
- Theme articles exploring important prayer topics.
- Connections to prayer resources available online.

Print subscription: $24.99
(includes digital version)

Digital subscription: $19.99

Church Prayer Leaders Network membership: $30 (includes print, digital, and CPLN membership benefits)

Subscribe now.
Order at www.prayerconnect.net or call 800-217-5200.